DINOSAUR OPERA

BY

S.P. SOMTOW

Dinosaur Opera

by S.P. Somtow
published by Diplodocus Press

Paperback ISBN: 978-1940999-36-4
Hardcover ISBN: 978-1940999-37-1

The text is by S.P. Somtow, which is the literary pseudonym of Somtow Sucharitkul

Illustrations prompted, selected, edited and overseen by Somtow Sucharitkul, who is a human being, with the assistance of (but not "generated by") AI, which is not a human being

© 2024 by Somtow Sucharitkul

Dedication

To Trisdee na Patalung
who would rehearse
a Mozart opera all day
then go home
and fall asleep
watching *Jurassic Park*
for the hundredth time…

WARNING

Some kids may think this little book
Is just a kind of hoax
Their parents might say they're too young
To understand the jokes

But wait a while, how time will fly!
Soon you'll be wiser, bolder,
It all will be as clear as crystal
When you're a little older.

Raptors in the House

My parents weren't that happy
When I came home from the park
My shoes and slacks were slick with slime
And it was getting dark

"We told you when we got you
Your own pet dinosaur
That your velociraptor
Can't traipse mud on the floor."

"You and your messy dino
Are driving us insane!
It's time you got some culture
Into that goofy brain

"That's why you're going with us
To the Opera Festival
While Rex stays in the Dino-Pound
Next to the shopping mall!"

I wish they'd understand
That pets are people too,
They can appreciate the opera
As much as me or you

And in a better world
Where we can co-exist
There won't be any problem
To get Rex on the list.

Don't get me wrong; this stuff is cool,
My uncle's a conductor
And when it comes to opera plots
He is a great instructor.

"The usual plot is, A loves B
Whose passion D then stokes
They sing some piercing, shrill top Cs
And then ... the lady croaks ..."

So, once it started, I soon drifted
Into a blissful slumber
My dream world filled with Singers
And Dinos without number

'Cos raptors can sing louder
Than any old soprano
And with the darkest villain
They can go *mano a mano*

Now, stories through my mind
Are streaming
Though slightly altered by
My dreaming....

The Magic Flute

A prince who falls in love
By looking at a picture;
A bird-man disobeying
The night-queen's strictest stricture

Three boys who flit about the stage
Dispensing sage advice;
A flute, and bells, and a bird-cage,
And brass chords that sound thrice

Meanwhile, it seems, the Wicked King
Was really only chillin'
And whaddya know! We soon find out
The Good Queen is the Villain

To get to win the one you love
Means passing an exam
The prince's friend flunks out, and gets
The booby prize ... yes, ma'am!

At last, the prince and princess pass
Through Water and through Fire
We know that they have aced the test
When Maestro cues the choir

The Birdman, sadly, didn't win
The maiden he had hoped;
Abracadacbra! Switch the girl!
Behold! - they just eloped!

Most PhDs cannot, it seems,
Unravel Mozart's knot
Only a kid would have the smarts
To just ignore the plot

Who understands *The Magic Flute?*
The story is notorious
I don't think Mozart gave a hoot
Because the music's glorious

AÏDA

Aïda may be just a slave
But where *she's* from, Dad's King;
Her love for top Egyptian brass
Is more than just a fling

Princess Amneris may know how
To walk like an Egyptian
but when she spots a rival
She sure has a conniption

It galls her even more to find
Her loved one does not heed her;
He looks right past her and declares:
"Take me to Aïda."

The noble Pharoah and his Child
Turn into jealous dweebs
When Egypt's armies all come trooping
Through the streets of Thebes

The Monarch says, "You've won the war
So now you get my Daughter!"
"But I'm in love with someone else,
I really shouldn't oughta!"

Torn 'twixt his land and his beloved,
His country he betrays —
Pharaoh decrees a breathless fate
For lovesick Radamès!

Now in a pyramid entombed
Are prince and princess proud,
They still might have some oxygen
Had they not sung so loud.

Cosi Fan Tutte

Two sisters of surpassing beauty
Switch boyfriends by mistake
Then realize it's the kind of dream
Where they don't want to wake

Now, Eighteenth Century Damsels
Are enlightened and urban
Yet their Beaux it seems, go in disguise
By slipping on a turban

But in the Seventeen Hundreds,
Love always bows to duty
The maid pretends to be a judge,
And says ... "Cosi fan tutte.*"

Which lady gets which gentleman?
And do the boys get jealous?
The experts say that both ways work,
And Mozart doesn't tell us.

* "They all do it"

LUCIA DI LAMMERMOOR

For women in Old Scotland
It really was a bad scene
One way to get attention?
Perform a Big Old Mad Scene

What of Lucia's complex plot?
Our memory's not so kind
That endless, stratospheric aria
Is all that comes to mind…

And a sextet — just one "momento"
You'll wonder where those hours went to.

The Ring of the Nibelungen

The head god, Wotan, ruins the world
And finds he has to wing it
It's basically "Lord of the Rings"
Except they have to sing it.

It's really, really, really long
It took the music world by storm
With dragons, dwarves, and talking birds
And fifteen hours to perform

We start beneath the River Rhine
A dwarf who's rather bold
He wants a mermaid for his moll
But ends up with some gold

The gold becomes a magic ring
Which bears a gruesome curse
If you possess it, you will die
If not, your fate is worse

The head god tries to fix this mess
And save the universe
By having lots and lots of kids
So one will flout the curse

Nine daughters called the Valkyries
Three daughters called the Norns
A grandson, Siegfried, good with swords
And great at blowing horns

It all goes wrong: Valhalla burns
The fire turns to flood
And heaven, earth, and all between
Become a pile of mud

The moral of this epic tale
Is something often told
Don't steal from mermaids or from dwarves
You'll end up with *fool's gold*.

Carmen

Now Carmen was a naughty girl
Who made her boyfriends fret so
She charmed the guys without high Cs
Because she was a mezzo

When Don José threw her in jail
For getting in a fight
She sang to him — he fell in love —
They ran off in the night

But though he sprung her from her cell
With swiftness and agility
Don José liked to cling, and soon
Became a liability

She didn't want to settle down
With someone unexciting
She had another guy in mind
Who majored in bull-fighting

So — A loves B and B loves C
Which often leads to crime —
The bull was merely in the way
Wrong place at the wrong time

What lessons do we learn from this?
In love, don't lose your brain
And if your fate made you a bull
Try not to live in Spain

Don Giovanni

Now Don Giovanni liked the ladies
But he was pretty cruel
To challenge Donna Anna's angry
Daddy to a duel

No matter who you think you are
Your past will always catch you
No matter if your nemesis
Is just a Singing Statue

LOHENGRIN

A Damsel is about to suffer
A dark and dismal fate
Astride a Swan, a Knight shows up
When it's almost too late

He rescues her, but he can't leave
She tells him, "Not so soon!
Thou needs must tarry here awhile —
The last swan left at noon."

ELISABETTA, REGINA D'INGHILTERRA

The Overture for *Elisabetta*
Regina d'Inghilterra
Was way too funny for the subject —
Said Jack*, "I've made an error."

"Aurelian of Palmyra?
Too serious it is still —
I'll just attach this ditty to
The Barber of Seville."

* *Giacchino Rossini, composer, liked to recycle his overtures.*

MADAM BUTTERFLY

The tale of Madam Butterfly
Is not what you'd call cheery
He loves her, leaves her, takes her kid,
She's left with hara-kiri!*

* It's more polite to say seppuku, but a lot harder to rhyme.

The Marriage of Figaro

She thinks that he will marry her,
Not knowing he's her son
Abandoned in an orphanage
and nurtured by a nun

Meanwhile the man who's suing him
Is actually his father
Who doesn't realize she's his ex ...
Are you confused yet? Rather!

He thinks he's chatting up the Maid
That she believes his lies
Not realizing that he is wooing
His own Wife, in *disguise*

Who's loved by a young Equerry
(Who's acted by a female)
"Be off to war!" the Count commands
"Don't even send an email!"

Barbarina and Susanna,
Marcellina, Rosina, and more...
The greedy count is not content
With two or three or four

It all comes out right in the end
Although it really shouldn't
The Countess grants the Cad forgiveness
I wonder why? *I* wouldn't.

SALOME

Salome was a princess
Whose dear mama misled
Into thinking dirty dancing
Was the way to get a head.

La Bohème and La Traviata

In both these tragic tales, the plot
Involves a Strange Presumption:
That women loved by many men
Must perish of Consumption.

Back to Reality

I woke up with a little start
To less than wild applause
Feeling the weight on my numb knees
Of Rex's razor claws

There's just too many operas!
I've only seen a few!
There are so many goofy plots
I'll have to write Book Two.

The Author

I live in a huge city
Inside a crowded nation
But also in the forest
Of my imagination

The Illustrator

I'm only a computer
I'm really not too smart
A human takes the "Ficial"
And turns it into "Art!"

A Note from the Author

Last year, I wrote *Dinosaur Symphony*, which is really a book to go along with a piece of music I am doing that teaches kids about the classical symphony orchestra by comparing each instrument to a different dinosaur. It was a one-off. But, for some reason ... it was more popular than my "real" books! *Dinosaur Ballet* was a hit too, so I suppose *Dinosaur Opera* was inevitable; I am, after all, an opera composer, and artistic director of an opera company.

But it caused more agony than the others, because opera plots can be pretty gruesome. And yet, they are really no gorier than the *real* Grimm's fairy tales. Cinderella's sisters having their eyes pecked out by crows, Sleeping Beauty assaulted in her sleep, Little Red Riding Hood being cut out of the wolf's tummy, and other horrors are as scary as anything in an opera. But, unlike with fairy tales, there are few "disneyfied" versions of opera plots. So, please, I urge caution, and have noted the "recommended age" for this book as somewhat higher than the others in the series.

Even so, every kid is different ... as is every grownup.

When the time came to illustrate the book, I turned to Artificial "Intelligence" for help, which was a little frustrating. It seems that AI knows less that most four-year-olds about what some dinosaurs looked like. It certainly has little clue about opera. A lot of tweaking and prodding, and the results are pretty entertaining. But please give the silicon guy a break. "Artificial" for sure; the jury is still out on "intelligence."

Honestly, this book shouldn't even exist. Is it even really a children's book? But I do know kids who go to the opera regularly,

Let's just say that it's not *just* a "children's book" but one that can be enjoyed by children of *all* ages. From kids with adult aspirations to adults in their second childhood, I hope this little foible of mine will be enjoyed by my fellow nerds throughout the world.

—S.P. Somtow

www.ingramcontent.com/pod-product-compliance
Lightning Source LLC
Chambersburg PA
CBHW041528070526
44586CB00002B/15